Christmas Delights

8 Early Elementary Christmas Carols
and Songs Arranged for Piano

Martha Mier

The beautiful sounds of Christmas music delight us each year anew, as we celebrate the season with time-honored Christmas carols and songs. *Christmas Delights*, Book One, contains eight of these favorite songs and carols arranged for the beginning pianist. Children love playing familiar melodies, and these Christmas solos will both delight and motivate them.

Each solo is wrtten with a single-line melody, divided between the hands, and is complete in itself. For a fuller, richer sound, the duet part for the teacher/parent may be added.

For a variety of your favorite Christmas music, *Christmas Delights*, Book One, will surely delight both performer and listener. Enjoy the music of the season!

Merry Christmas!

Martha M.

Away in a Manger 8

Deck the Halls 16

First Noel, The 12

I Am So Glad on Christmas Eve 6

Jolly Old Saint Nicholas 4

Silent Night .10

We Three Kings of Orient Are 2

We Wish You a Merry Christmas 14

Alfred

We Three Kings of Orient Are

John Henry Hopkins, Jr.
Arr. by Martha Mier

DUET PART (Student plays 1 octave higher.)

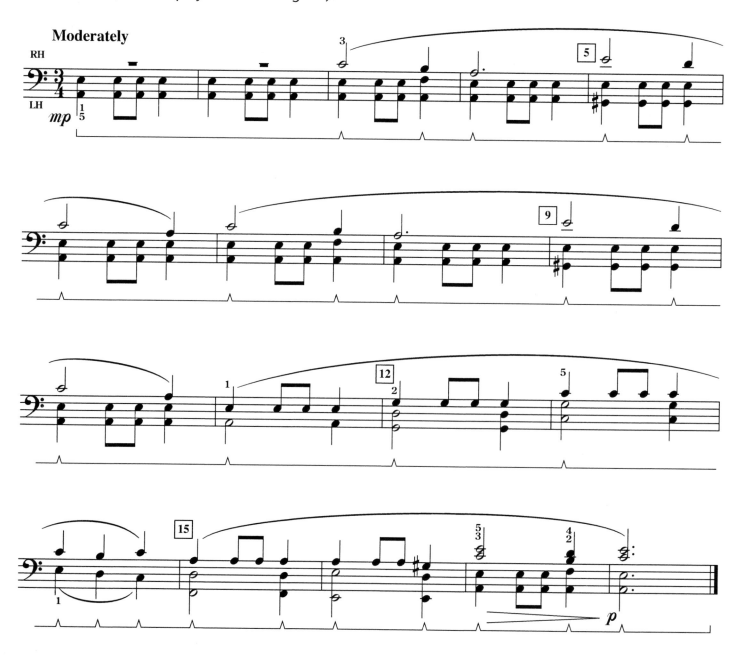

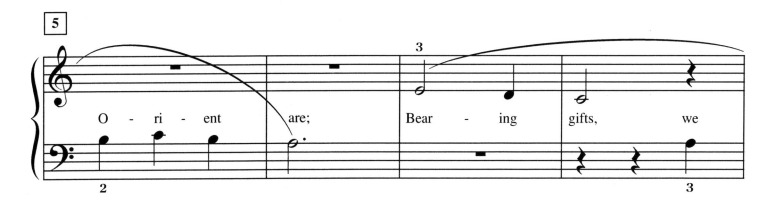

O – ri – ent are; Bear – ing gifts, we

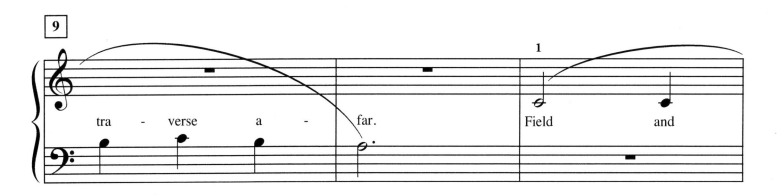

tra – verse a – far. Field and

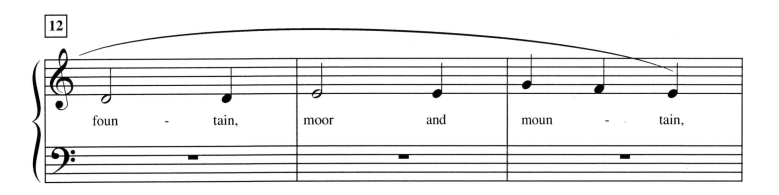

foun – tain, moor and moun – tain,

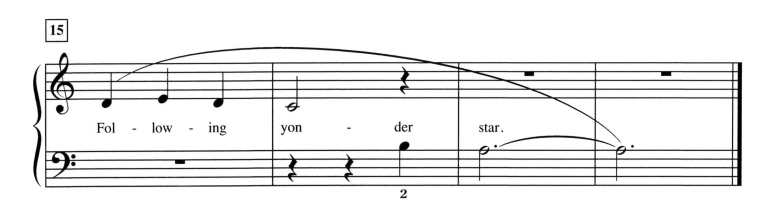

Fol – low – ing yon – der star.

Jolly Old Saint Nicholas

Traditional
Arr. by Martha Mier

Happily

Jol - ly old Saint Nich - o - las, lean your ear this

DUET PART (Student plays 1 octave higher.)

molto rit.

mp

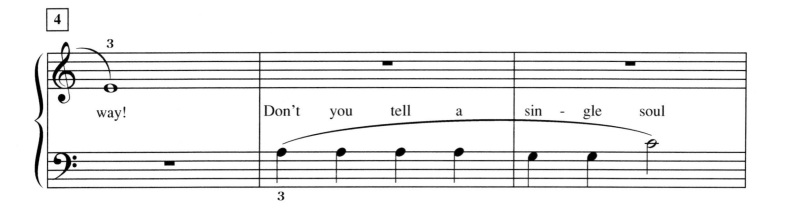

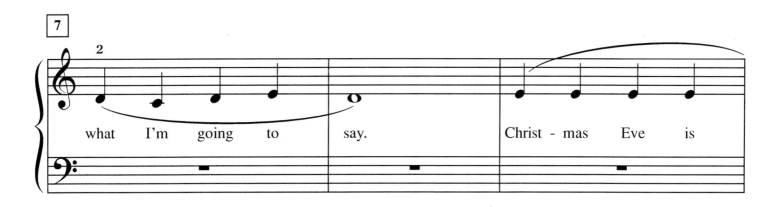

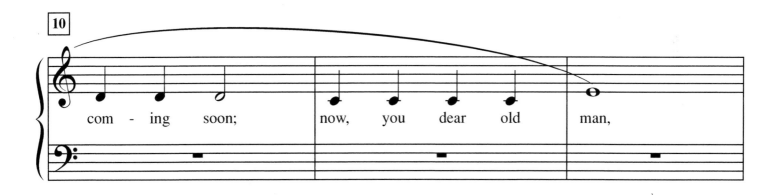

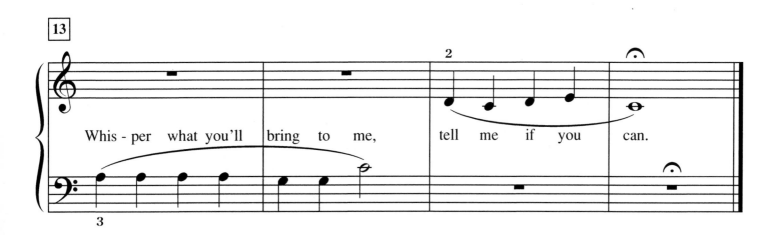

I Am So Glad on Christmas Eve

Traditional Norwegian Carol
Arr. by Martha Mier

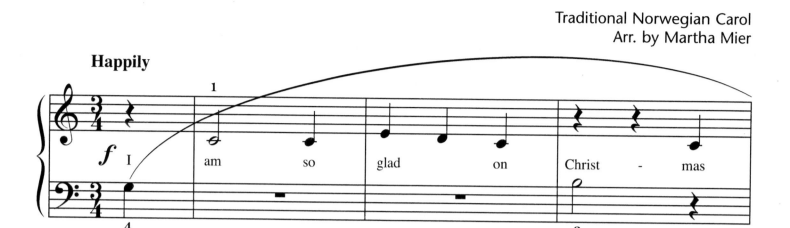

DUET PART (Student plays 1 octave higher.)

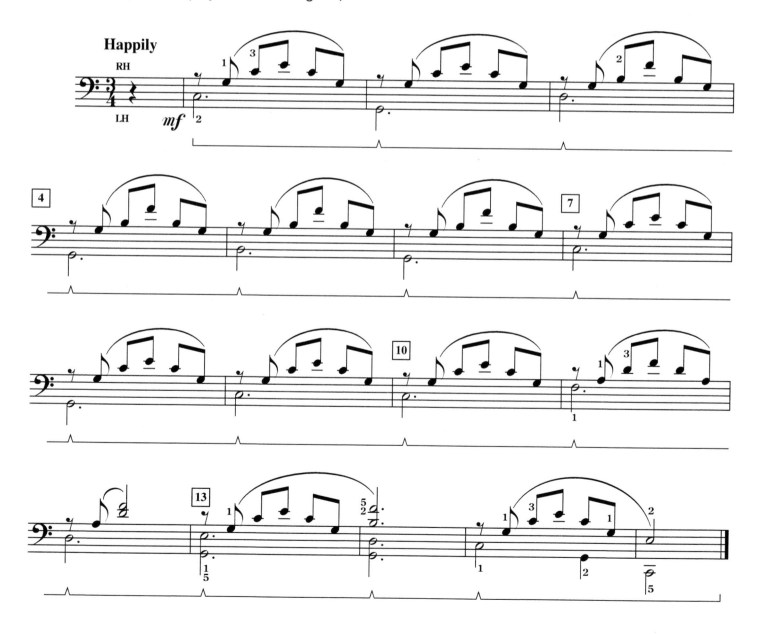

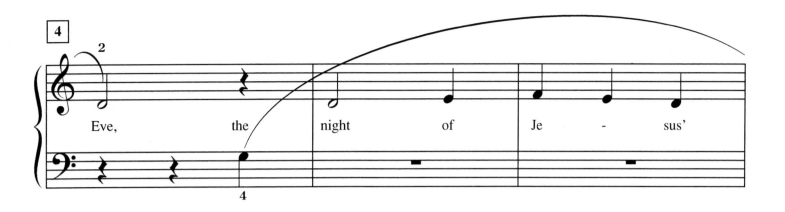

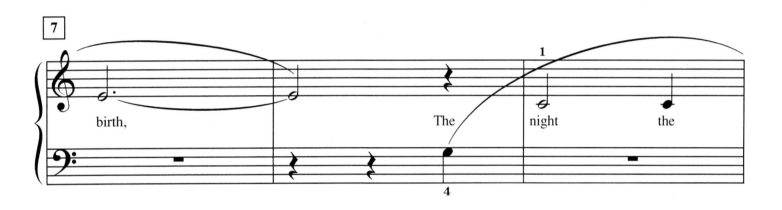

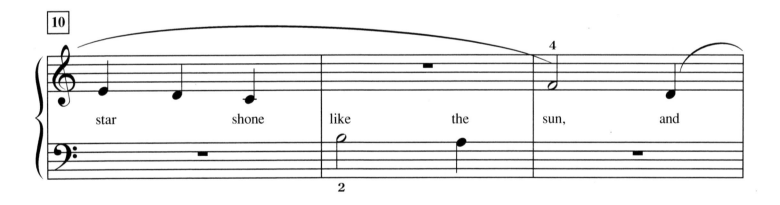

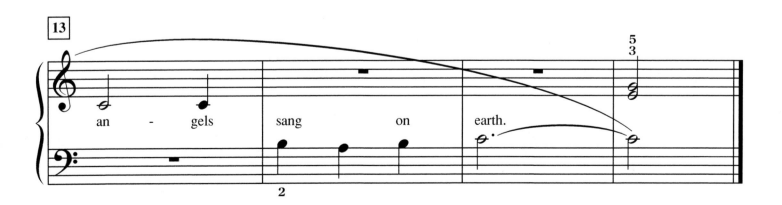

Away in a Manger

James R. Murray
Arr. by Martha Mier

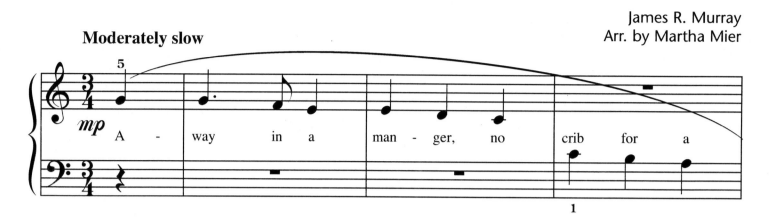

DUET PART (Student plays 1 octave higher.)

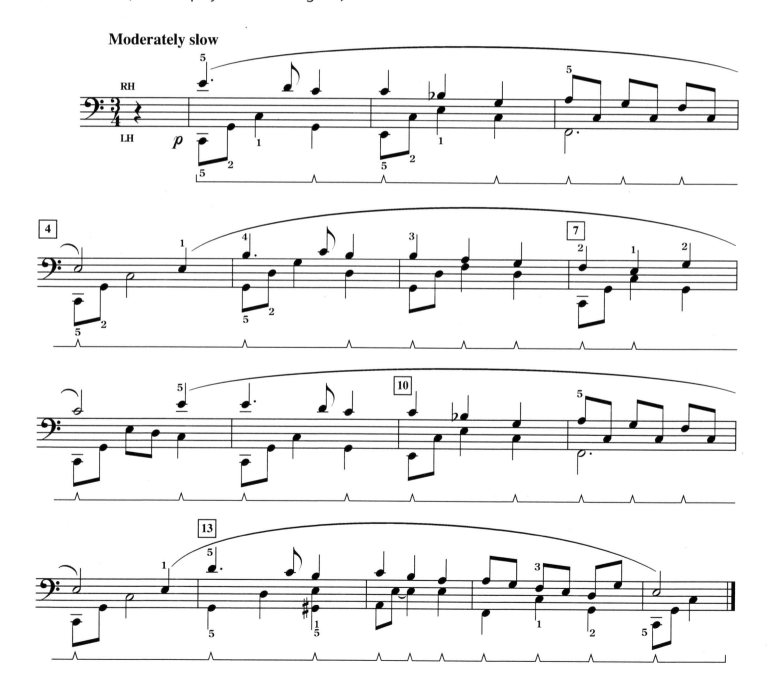

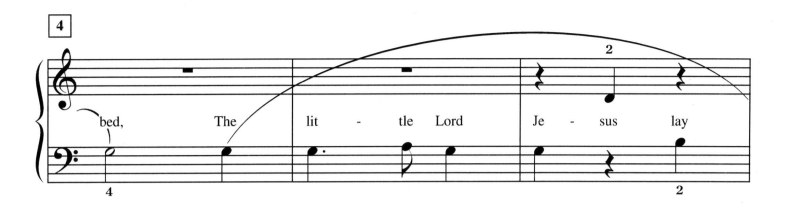

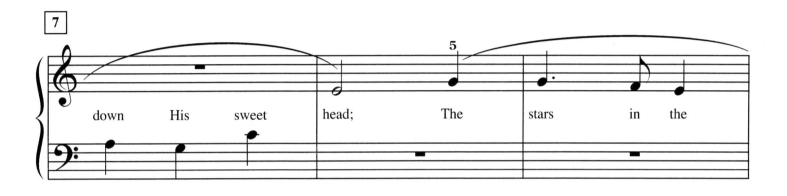

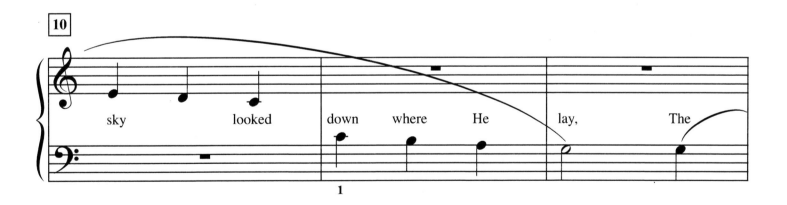

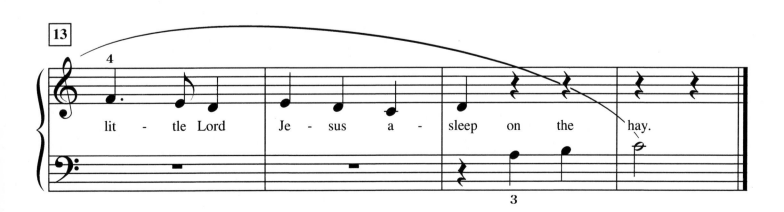

Silent Night

Franz Grüber
Arr. by Martha Mier

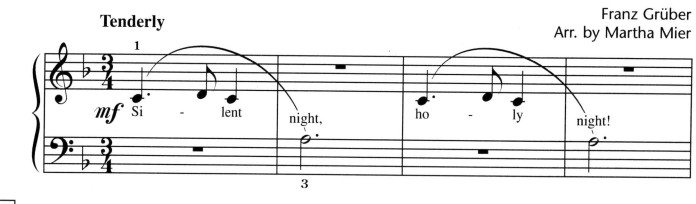

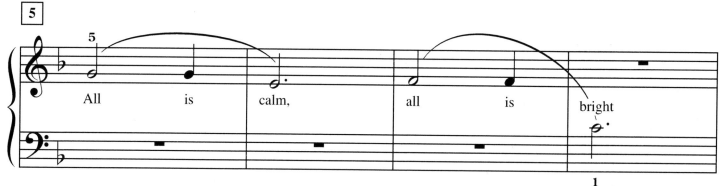

DUET PART (Student plays 1 octave higher.)

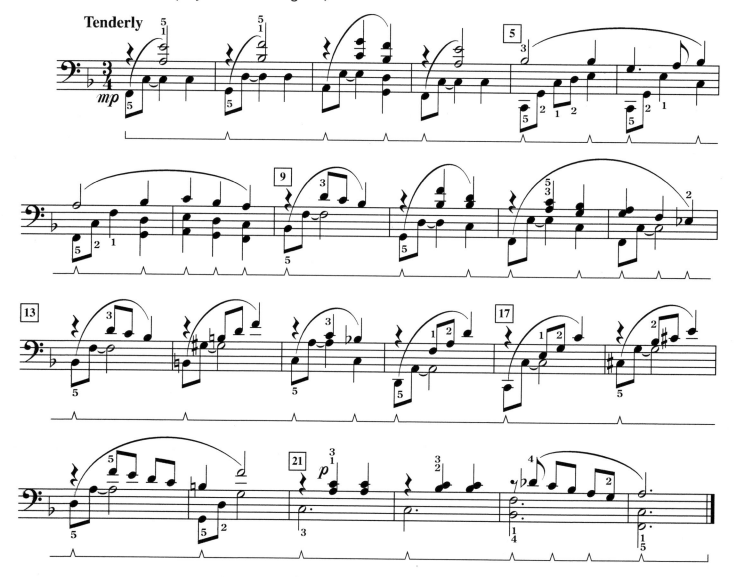

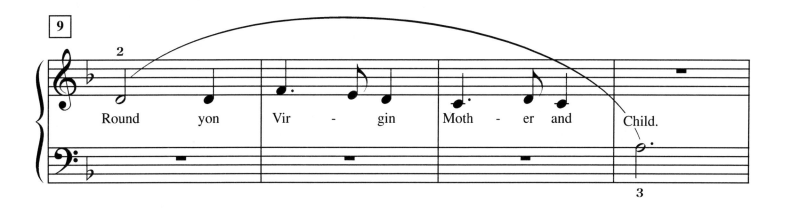

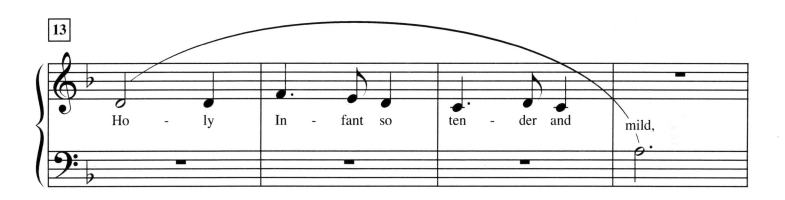

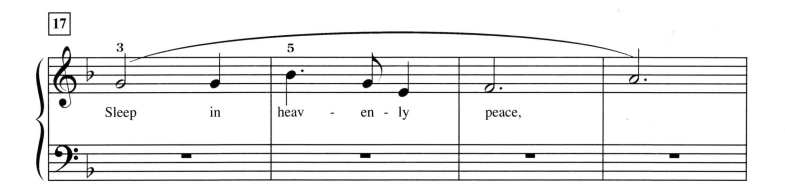

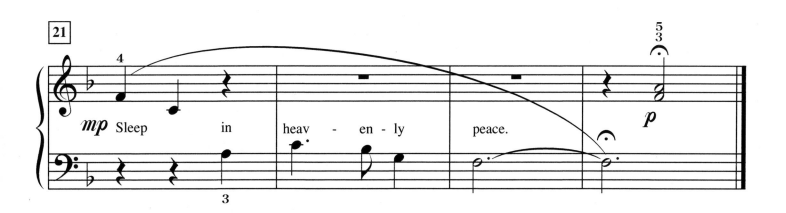

The First Noel

Traditional English Carol
Arr. by Martha Mier

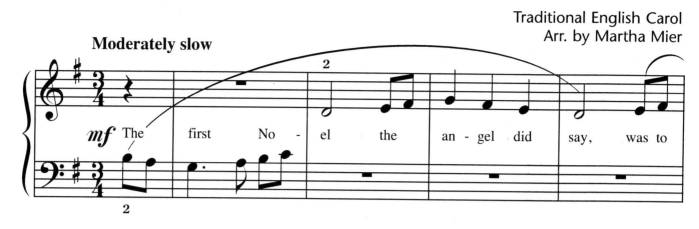

Moderately slow

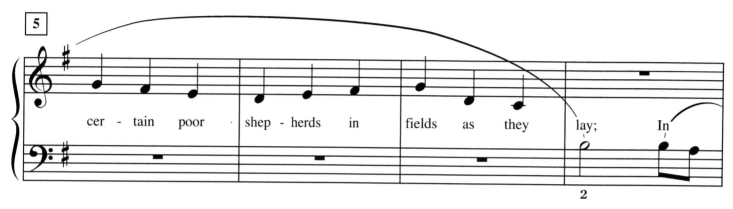

mf The first No - el the an - gel did say, was to

cer - tain poor shep - herds in fields as they lay; In

DUET PART (Student plays 1 octave higher.)

Moderately slow

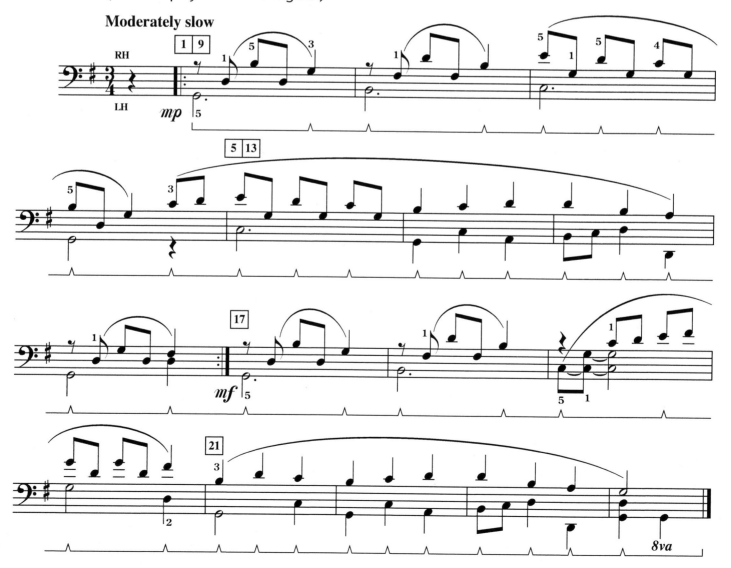

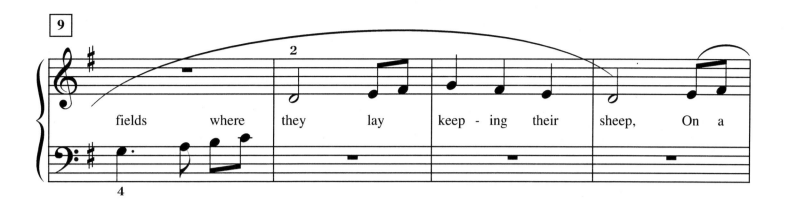

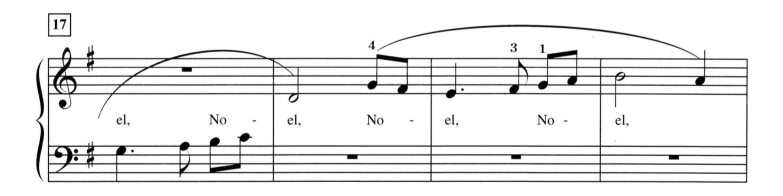

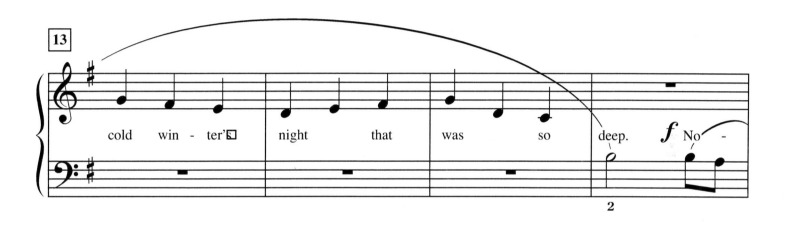

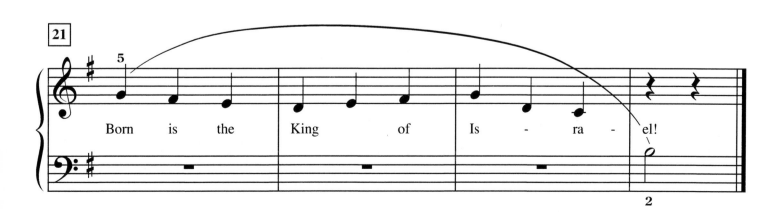

We Wish You a Merry Christmas

Traditional
Arr. by Martha Mier

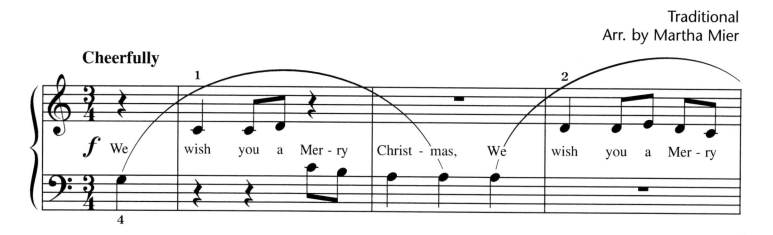

DUET PART (Student plays 1 octave higher.)

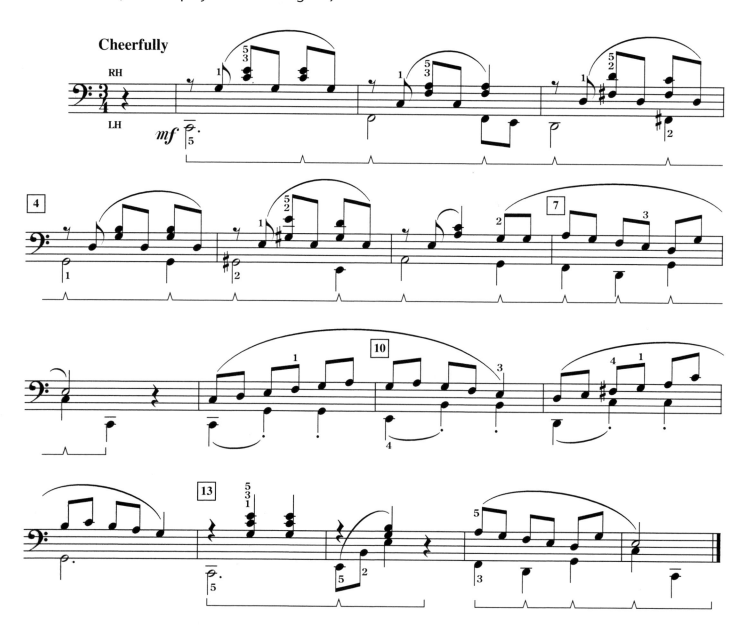

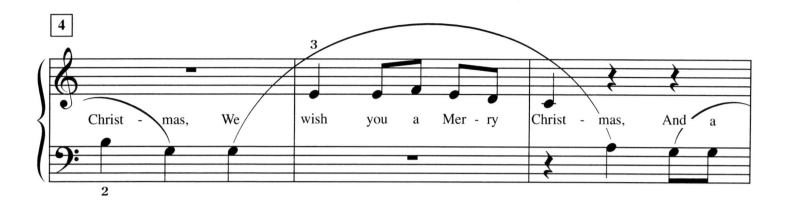

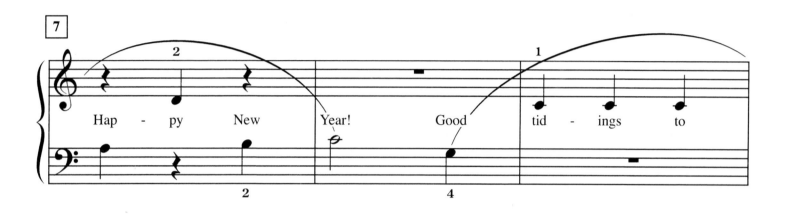

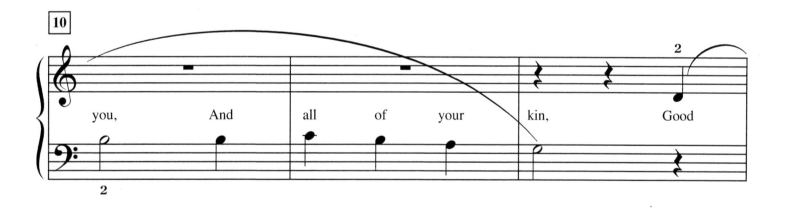

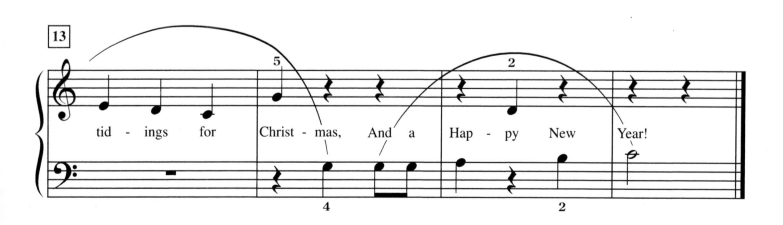

Deck the Halls

Traditional
Arr. by Martha Mier

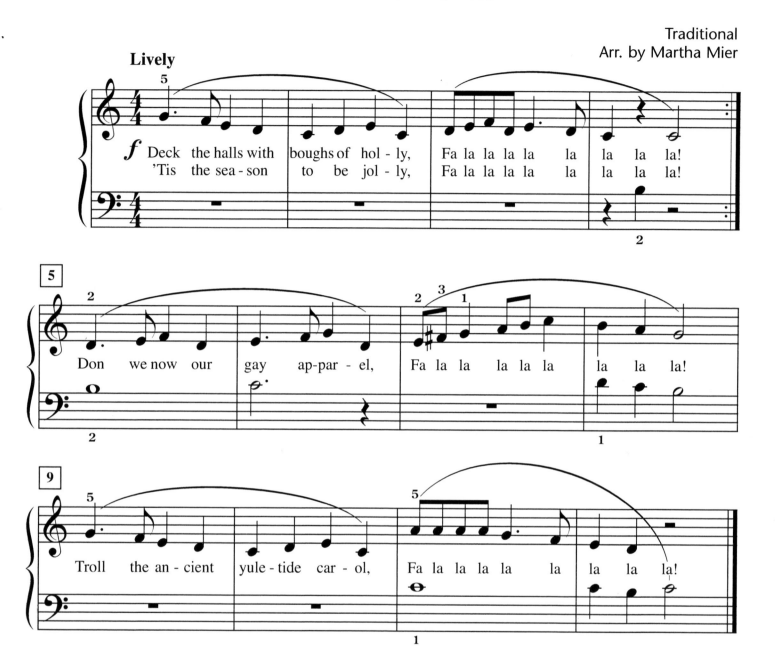

DUET PART (Student plays 1 octave higher.)

Christmas Piano Music from Alfred

Christmas Collections

Early Elementary
Christmas Carol Activity Book, Pre-Reading *(Kowalchyk/Lancaster)* 18197
Christmas Festival, Book 1 *(Kowalchyk/Lancaster)* 6012
My First Christmas Carols *(Kowalchyk/Lancaster)* 233
Nutcracker Activity Book, The, Pre-Reading *(Gerou)* 21320

Early Elementary/Elementary
Christmas Carol Activity Book 1 *(Kowalchyk/Lancaster)* 18198
Christmas Delights, Book 1 *(Mier)* 20737
Nutcracker Activity Book, The, Book 1 *(Gerou)* 22432

Elementary
Christmas Festival, Book 2 *(Kowalchyk/Lancaster)* 6044
First Favorite Christmas Carols *(Olson)* 2539
Let's Celebrate The Nutcracker! *(Johnson)* 19709
Simply Classic Christmas, A *(Goldston)* 17384

Elementary/Late Elementary
Christmas Carol Activity Book 2 *(Kowalchyk/Lancaster)* 18810
Christmas on the Jazzy Side *(Aaronson)* 19746
Simply Classic Nutcracker, A *(Goldston)* 18077

Late Elementary
Christmas Delights, Book 2 *(Mier)* 21340
Christmas Festival, Book 3 *(Kowalchyk/Lancaster)* 6590
Christmas Miniatures, Book 1 *(Goldston)* 6903
Christmas Songs & Solos, Book 1 *(Goldston)* 6048
Story of Christmas, The *(Olson)* 800
We Wish You a Merry Christmas *(White-Hayward)* 11743

Late Elementary/Early Intermediate
Christmas Cheer, Book 1 *(Mier)* 6680
Easiest Christmas Carols *(Small)* 660
Merry Christmas to All *(Garcia)* 18825
Merry Little Christmas, A *(Renfrow)* 16883
Nutcracker Suite, The *(Kowalchyk/Lancaster)* 16876
Simply Classic Nutcracker Duets *(Goldston)* 21343
Stories of the Great Christmas Carols *(Montgomery/Renfrow)* 21391

Early Intermediate
Christmas, Christmas, Christmas *(Ray)* 11740
Christmas Delights, Book 3 *(Mier)* 21341
Christmas Festival, Book 4 *(Kowalchyk/Lancaster)* 6599
Christmas Lites—Modern & Bright *(Aaronson)* 11735
Christmas Miniatures, Book 2 *(Goldston)* 14708
Christmas Songs & Solos, Book 2 *(Goldston)* 6591
Simply Christmas *(Ray)* 1188
Something Special for Christmas *(Hartsell)* 6015
We Wish You a Jazzy Christmas *(Rollin)* 16882

Early Intermediate/Intermediate
Christmas Story, The *(Garcia)* 20738

Intermediate
Carols for the Season, Organ *(Page)* 12231
Christmas Carol Songbook, The *(Small)* 662
Christmas Cheer, Book 2 *(Mier)* 6697
Christmas from the Heart, Book 1 *(Massoud)* 14695
Christmas from the Heart, Book 2 *(Massoud)* 16879
Christmas Holiday *(Palmer)* 658
Christmas Impressions, Book 1 *(Rollin)* 6566
Christmas Impressions, Book 2 *(Rollin)* 6682
Christmas Medleys & Variations *(Rollin)* 21342
Christmas Pleasures *(Rollin)* 11744
Christmas Silhouettes *(Alexander)* 6006
Christmas to Remember, A *(Hartsell)* 6046
Family Christmas Sing-Along, A *(Ray)* 6687
Gifts of the Season *(Wells)* 18753
Notebook for Saint Nicholas *(Jancewicz)* 18076
Ragtime Christmas, A *(Renfrow)* 18755
Sounds Christmas *(Olson)* 2390
Spotlight on Christmas *(Rollin)* 18761

Intermediate/Late Intermediate
Christmas Inspirations, Book 1 *(Tingley)* 17383
Christmas Kaleidoscope, Book 1 *(Mier)* 16878

Christmas Kaleidoscope, Book 2 *(Mier)* 18754
Christmas Stylings—Modern & Bright, Book 1 *(Aaronson)* 6014
Nutcracker Suite, The *(Kowalchyk/Lancaster)* 6900
Virtuosic Christmas Performer, The *(Goldston)* 20741

Late Intermediate
Christmas Collage, A, Book 1 *(Hartsell)* 6681
Christmas Collage, A, Book 2 *(Hartsell)* 6699
Christmas Collection, A, Book 1 *(Renfrow)* 6047
Christmas Splendor *(Alexander)* 16918

Late Intermediate/Early Advanced
Christmas Collection, A, Book 2 *(Renfrow)* 6549
Christmas Fantasy, A *(Alexander)* 6559
Christmas Stylings—Modern & Bright, Book 2 *(Aaronson)* 6045

Early Advanced
Come to the Manger *(Page)* 14711

Early Advanced/Advanced
Christmas with Style *(Ray)* 659
Mendelssohn—Six Christmas Pieces, Op. 72 *(Palmer)* 1958
More Christmas with Style *(Ray)* 1189
Tchaikovsky—The Nutcracker Suite *(Hinson)* 4856
Variations on Adeste Fidelis *(Taylor/Krauss/Hinson)* 11131

Advanced
Joy to the World *(Larson)* 22429

Christmas Duets

Early Elementary
Duets for Christmas Lovers, Book 1 *(Goldston)* 6663

Early Elementary/Elementary
First Favorite Christmas Duets *(Olson)* 863

Elementary
Duets for Christmas Lovers, Book 2 *(Goldston)* 6664
Up on the Housetop *(Goldston)* 5459

Late Elementary
Christmas for Two *(Ray)* 205
Christmas Tree-O!, A (1 Piano, 6 Hands) *(Alexander)* 14515
Duets for Christmas Lovers, Book 3 *(Goldston)* 6665
Holly and the Ivy, The (1 Piano, 6 Hands) *(Alexander)* 14235
'Twas the Night Before… *(Alexander)* 6683

Late Elementary/Early Intermediate
Simply Classic Nutcracker Duets *(Goldston)* 21343

Early Intermediate
Away in a Manger *(Tingley)* 18974
Coventry Carol, The *(Alexander)* 8425
What Child Is This? *(Massoud)* 18975

Intermediate
Carol of the Bells *(Rollin)* 18976
Ding Dong Merrily on High *(Mier)* 18977
Magic of Christmas, The, Book 1 *(Alexander)* 653
Magic of Christmas, The, Book 2 *(Alexander)* 235
Silent Night *(Aaronson)* 18978

Intermediate/Late Intermediate
Nutcracker Suite for Two, The *(Rollin)* 16919

Late Intermediate
Magic of Christmas, The, Book 3 *(Alexander)* 21389

Early Advanced
God Rest Ye Merry, Gentlemen *(Alexander)* 18979

Early Advanced/Advanced
Reinecke—Nutcracker and the Mouse King, Op. 46 *(Hinson)* 2275
Tchaikovsky—The Nutcracker Suite *(Hinson)* 4858

Christmas Recital Suites

Late Intermediate
Three Moods for Christmas *(Aaronson)* 22456

ISBN-10: 0-7390-2247-4
ISBN-13: 978-0-7390-2247-4

alfred.com

20737

USA

ISBN 0-7390-2247-4

ACCENT ON
Christmas & Holiday
ENSEMBLES

Duets and trios for flexible instrumentation
correlated with **ACCENT ON ACHIEVEMENT**, Book 1

John
O'Reilly
and
Mark
Williams

Alfred